BLACK HEART SHINING

Copyright @ 1996 by T. Rhein

All rights reserved. No part of this book may be reproduced or transmitted in any form or by any means, electronic or mechanical, including photo-copying, recording, or by any information storage and retrieval system, without permission in writing from the publisher.

Published by Luna Daeolin Inc.
PO Box 9134
Cincinnati, Ohio 45209

Manufactured in the United States of America
This is a First Edition Copy. This is one of only 500 copies printed.
Library of Congress Cataloging-in-Publication Data is available upon request.

ISBN 0-9663037-0-9

Book Number: __248__

Dad,

Took a little longer than you wanted, probably not any longer than you expected. Sorry you missed it.

T. Rhein

THE FINE ART OF UNDERSTANDING

Just like a man
who never changes the toilet paper roll
or leaves just one sheet,
you repeat and repeat
words never heard.
No need to listen.

INTERESTING REACTION, BUT WHAT DOES IT MEAN?

To find a place in this world...
equations, chemistry, Buddha, soul,
answers to questions
unasked, unanswered.

Still blood flows through,
its secrets willed.
Those visions want reality
unbound by environment
or personality.

I am simple.
I would find God in these moments
of doubt, uncertainty
about purpose.

The beauty of words
cannot spare me this loneliness.

The cricket outside in darkness
stops calling.

Dew collects,
the morning comes,
still moving.

BOBBY

A blue-eyed babe's cradle
rocked and swayed.
His parents schemed,
if we could sell that smile...
beauty pageants, commercials, TV,
maybe even the big screen
they dared to dream.
The magic kingdom beckoned
in that innocent sort of way,
on those fairy tale streets
every child can have their day.
So Bobby's face
would fill the big screen.
Bigger checks, bigger expectations,
everything his parents wanted;
the time of his life
he couldn't save.

That image of eternal youth
captured on film.
It was my favorite movie.

He lay there for days,
broken heart it seems.
Shooting up started an end to that dream.
Bobby said, "Put all my spare time in my arm.
Tinkerbell had nothing on me;
that magic in the night,
took comfort in her charms."

They say he was the greatest child find.
In a tenement house
a corpse waits for a name.
That face looks familiar.
Needle marks shot in the dark.
There was a price to fame.

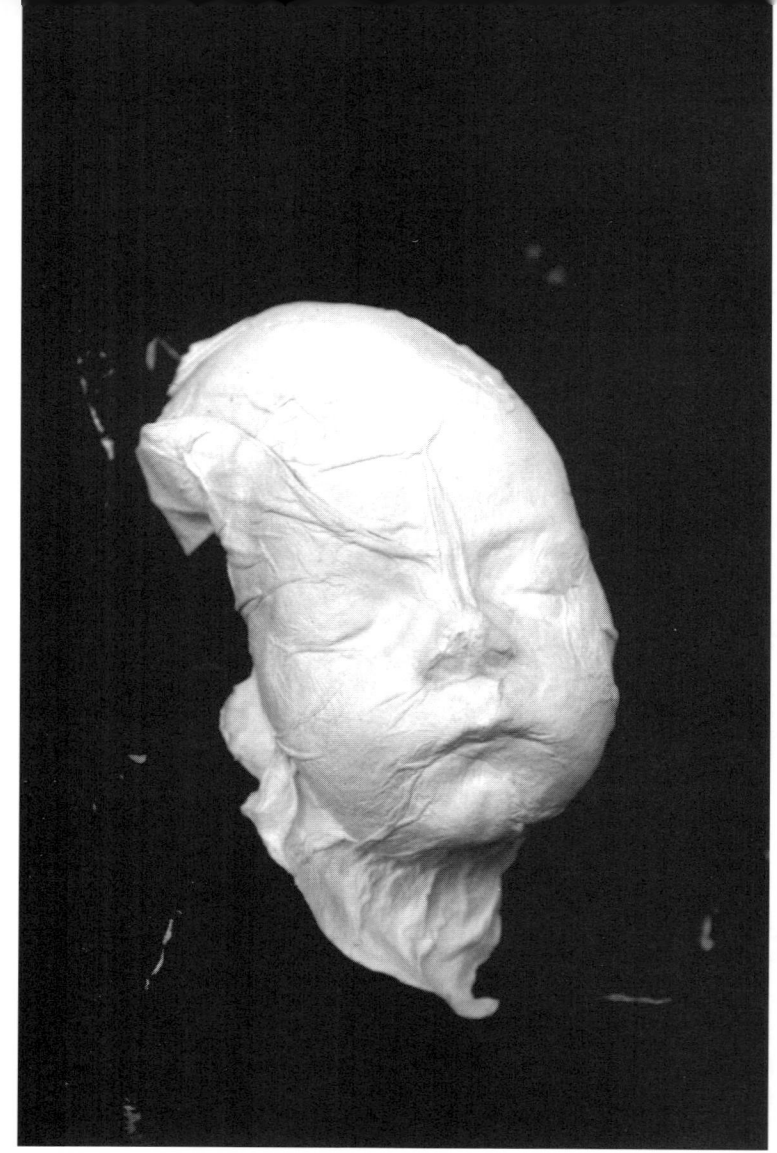

A FACE TO CALL MY OWN

I don't know my father.
Only time I've seen his face is mine.
My momma just sits there tight-lipped.

"Isn't all I've done for you enough?"

No, Momma. Every man has a time
he needs to hear his old man say,
"I couldn't be more proud of you, son,
than I am today."

We never played ball,
never whistled at the same pair of legs.
I never felt his punch or his hug,
never felt anything at all.
Just a shadow of a man I never met.
Just the features of a man I never saw…
and yet I am my father's son.

Some things must be the same.
The way I walk, deliver a line,
the emptiness inside as time goes by.
All I've got is his name, and a strong urge
to know why he left.

Pop, if you're out there
living with the memory of a kiss,
if you've ever wondered what became of a
chance encounter that sealed
momma's lips . . .

your boy's a grown man with kids of his own
and the need to understand the roots
of the seed you've sown.

Dad, phone home.
Please don't leave me unknown.

Delilah Wallenda

Every step death waits.
Lost
some folks I dearly loved this way.
Thrill as a way of life,
life on the high wire.

I balance it in my hands,
lose track of the hours.
Where faith is your guide,
God is the light that leads.
There is no fear,
just belief.

Those moments of clarity,
where your will
is your reality.

I walk above this earth, free.

THE GULF

Slicing sweltering heat.
Bullets fly,
death whistling her call.

On the killing floor,
with only seconds to decide,
your mind seeks out beliefs,
skin and bones and thoughts of why?

Standing there, a face of fear
defying sand that tears and sunders,
God's open hand to rise above
the shrieking sound of a distant thunder.

Night offers no retreat.
The letters from home paint distant scenes
of quieter skies over fields of need;
their cheerful words can't hide their concerns.
I feel their apprehension with every page...
war's the same in any age,
loved ones wanting their loved ones
to come home.

Yet tonight I lie far from that home,
uncertainty hangs with this loneliness.
Thinking 'bout the land of the free,
the life I've led,
where it could end.

Pray to God as this evening fades
that I'll not return in pieces
to the home of the brave.

Bar Harbor

Brine hangs sentence.
Ankle wreathes, ocean kisses...
fifty two degrees - penetrating
exposed bone, pale flesh.

Can you be cold and alive?

Immense endless rhythms,
shore, water, stone, sand.

Tides,
in and out of our lives.

The silence inside.
Breathing in water,
your body remembers
the expulsion at birth.
Tadpoles understand
transformation of
spirit.
Some shed skin.

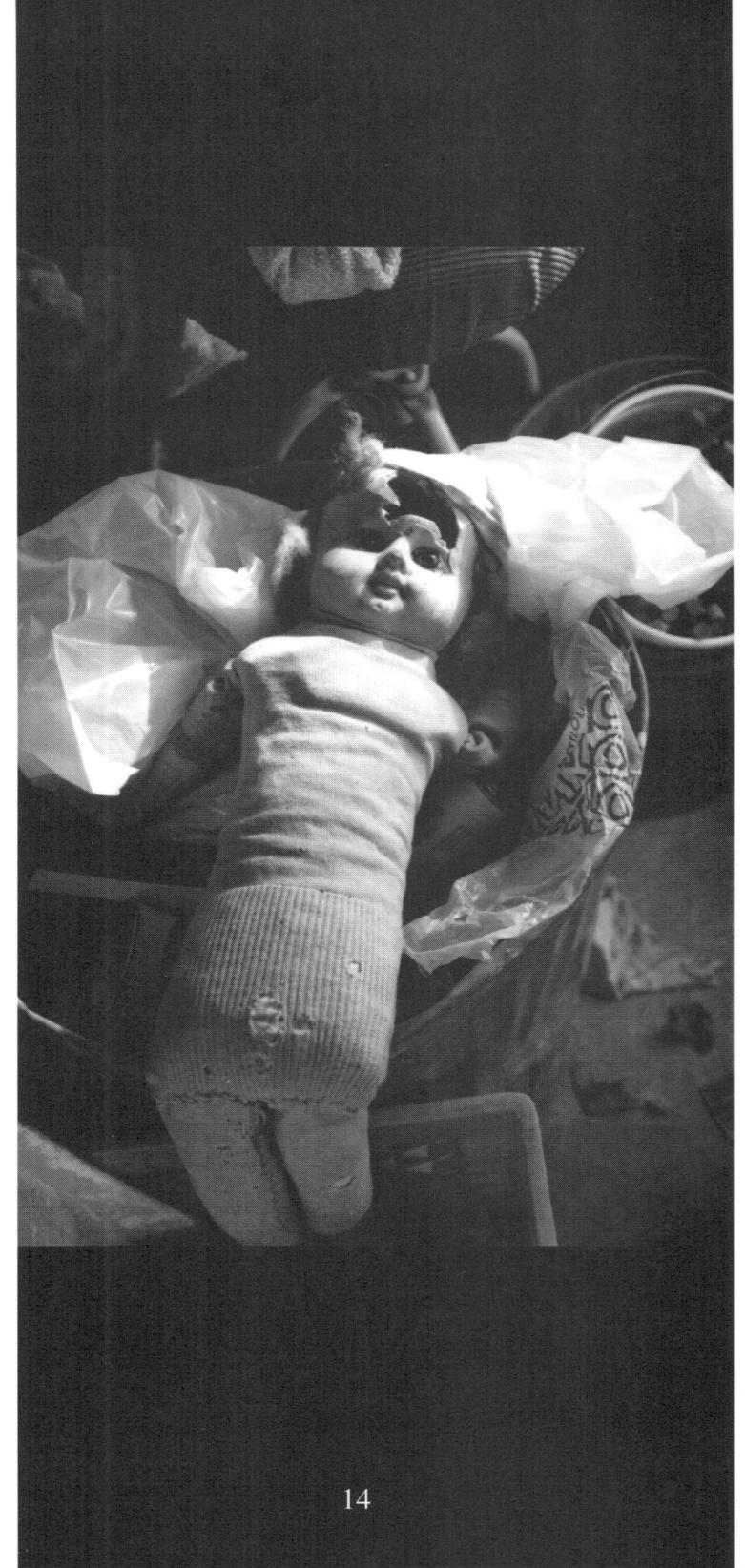

Photo by Margaret Rhein

THE GOLDEN ARCHES

THE CALL CAME IN - 4:15 A.M.
TWO ADDICTS IN THE BACK AND
THE WAIL OF A BABY.
I LIFTED HER INTO MY ARMS,
BODY VIOLENTLY SHAKING,
THE LIFE EBBING RIGHT OUT.

I THOUGHT, WHAT KIND OF WORLD ARE WE CREATING
JUST WAITING FOR A CHECK?

PREYING MANTIS APPROACHES,
HER CLOTHES TATTERED.
WITH A FLICK OF THE SWITCH
THE DARKNESS SCATTERS, REVEALING
A QUIVERING VOICE, EYES VACANT STILL
PANIC BREAKS THROUGH, UNBIDDEN FEAR.
I KNEW SHE WAS CRACKED.

JUST WAITING FOR A CHECK.

THE BABY'S BOTTOM WAS BLISTERED,
THE PLACE STANK OF SHIT.
MY STOMACH WAS TURNING TO SEE LIFE
OR LACK OF COME TO THIS.
THAT BABY DIED CRADLED IN MY ARMS.

MOMMA, LOOKING AT ME WITH HER ONE
REVIVING EYE, SAID,
"DO YOU THINK THEY'LL FIND OUT
'FORE THE CHECK'S BEEN MAILED?
I NEED IT SO BAD."
HER MOUTH TRIED TO SMILE.

I never thought I could feel this way…
so angry, so cold.
What is it? The system,
or a game to played?
Would it have been right
to end it there and then?
Or was her life just like that baby's,
over before it began?
Knowing a life of desperation remains
for those in these straits,
creating a cycle, I suspect,
a cycle of hopelessness and blame
that leaves a hand out to stop the pain.

Just waiting for a check.

Took that lost soul through the door.
"Don't worry 'bout that one,
I can always make more."

WHERE THE WRITTEN WORD TAKES US

The plagiarist,
lips sporting a scar
so thin you could brush it away
with a finger,
moves them; his tongue
slithers inviting.
Out of the darkness,
out of the scant light of his mouth,
as if their time on earth were that brief,
that dimly illuminated,
words appear.
He gives them freely,
knowing worry is nine-tenths of suffering.
"I'm sorry," he offers.

I had to try.

                                              Some images supplied by
                                              John Irving

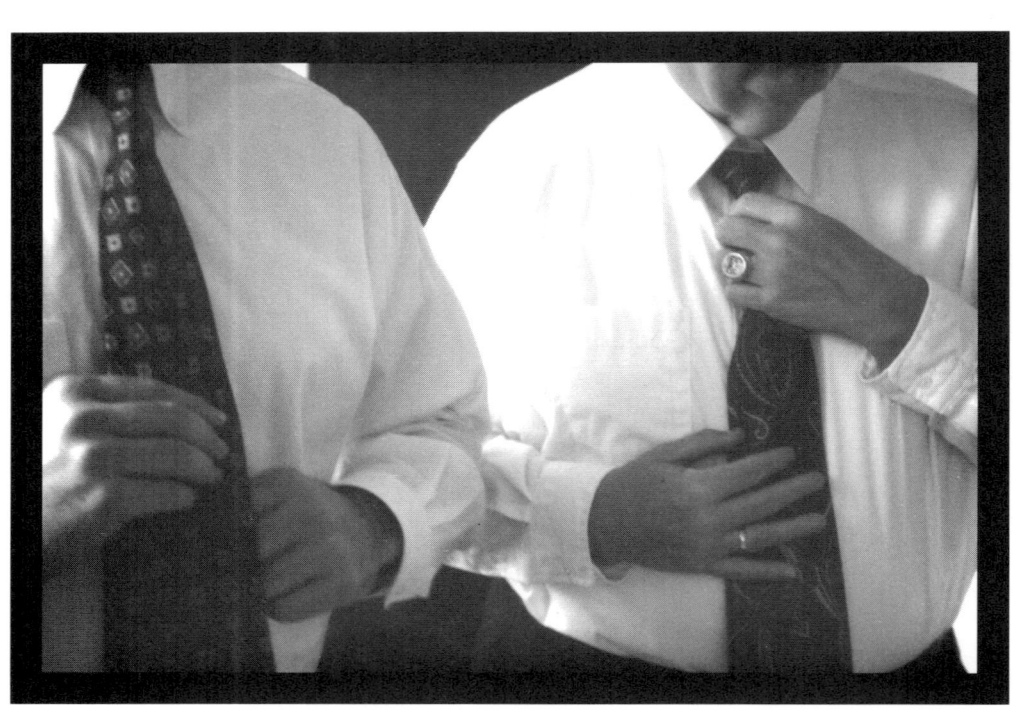

JUST BUSINESS

54,
THIS TIE HAS SEEN MANY MORNINGS;
CROSS, KNOT, BOW.
HE PUTS THE BUTT UNDER HIS HEEL.
"COFFEE, BLACK."

"YOU KNOW HOW WE FEEL ABOUT YOU.
YOU'VE BUILT THIS BUSINESS WITH YOUR OWN
STYLE, YOUR OWN TIME, AND YOU'VE BEEN
VERY SUCCESSFUL.
THINGS CHANGE;
YOUR NUMBERS ARE DOWN,
NOTHING PERSONAL,
JUST BUSINESS."
FEAR IS SUCH A POWERFUL MOTIVATOR.

"SOMETHING'S WRONG, I KNOW IT. WHAT IS IT?"
"NOTHING, HONEY, JUST BUSINESS."

"YOU LOST YOUR JOB. OH, JESUS, WHAT ARE WE GOING TO DO?"

"I THINK I'LL LOOK FOR MY GUTS SINCE THEY WERE
JUST RIPPED OUT.
ALL THOSE YEARS, GONE IN A FIFTEEN MINUTE MINUTE.
I SHOULD NEVER HAVE BOUGHT THE MAZDA,
CHRISTOPHER'S TUITION IS DUE,
AT LEAST ANNE'S WEDDING WAS LAST YEAR.
I GOT A YEAR'S SEVERANCE. CHRIST, WHAT A WORD."

COAT LEFT HANGING OVER THE BACK OF A CHAIR,
KEYS TOSSED ON THE DINING ROOM TABLE;
GOING ABOUT MY FATHER'S BUSINESS.

CORE

I want to peel you
till naked you stand.

Stripped of your defenses,
the core of who you are
in my hands.

Watching you rise
to the hunger in my eyes,
feeling each thrust
of pleasure inside.

The dizzying power of love
your body expresses.
The laughter and joy
in each of your caresses.

I melt for you.

Thinking about the distance,
lost addresses.

15 SECONDS

Peering between the sun's morning glare
I see you
in your rearview mirror.
Looking back,
just your eyes,
  not your lips.
With unspoken wishes, I imagine
  just a wisp of your hair
curled and tangled.

The distance between us as you
pull away,
two strangers reflecting,
15 seconds of time.

I notice the cat,
thinking, "Somebody's lost a loved one;
roadside victim."
Suddenly it lifts its head,
not dead yet.

Global wars, plane crash victims, Nicole Brown Simpson,
slash through my head
as angels, rising and falling issue
sounds from the car radio.

This life.
I kept driving.

MY BOY

Cherries,
picked while still blossoming.
On a September's starry ride,
the sky was twirling.

Late night homecoming
we went with the moment,
without doubt;
filling someone else's needs,
that babe was conceived.

Choices roar through
this silent night.

Sand foams beneath my wings.
No longer innocent,
not old enough to forget fear,
giving up
all those dreams.

The angels make believe a better place.
Heaven as earth
in my baby's face.

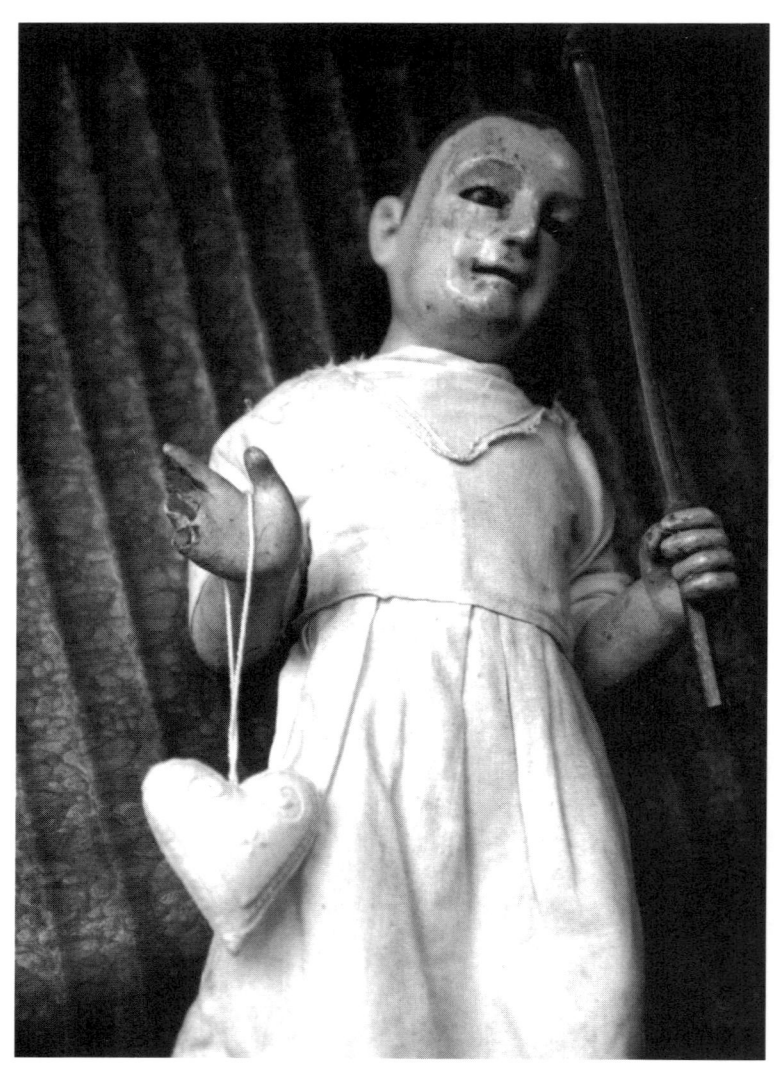

THE CONFESSION

A memory-
six, maybe seven
"Let me play with you,
it feels like heaven."
Don't remember any angels singing,
just his long low moans.
"If you tell anyone, I'll kill you.
They'll just think you're queer,
I'll tell them it's true."
The priest hears all my fears.
"Three Our Fathers, three Hail Marys."
Cast-out.
If God knows, does God care?
I prayed. Over and over.
Ten, in the alleyway, was the second time.
Cutting the slit, forcing his way in.
"Good to see you again, boy."
Tears didn't matter,
brain screaming in silence.
"I can't wait to do you again, son."
That laugh.
If God knows, does God care?

How bad this faith has been shaken.
What's your out when all the good
has been taken?
Alone and empty; so silent.
And I scrub and I scrub
but I can't get clean.
These days you can't touch me.
Innocent eyes are blind; I see
words more than deeds.
A lifetime guilt that drives me to my knees.
"Oh, Lord, please tell me this life was Hell."

THE TIME IN BETWEEN

"I hope this won't change our relationship."
I wanted to love him
The way someone else
I loved
Loved him.

I can't.
His world of intimacy,
Woody conversations,
Small places, moments,
Exist for us only as memories.
He thinks he's Robert Frost.
"That part of America should be preserved, I think.
Towns where things still grow,
Folks still spend evenings murmuring
Under porch lights."

I ran as quickly as possible
Into the time in between
Life and its closure.
Leaving youth.
The horses greeted me at the fence,
The comfort of stars.

Paint peeling from old playground toys.
Pursuing what could have been.
Words echo haunting.

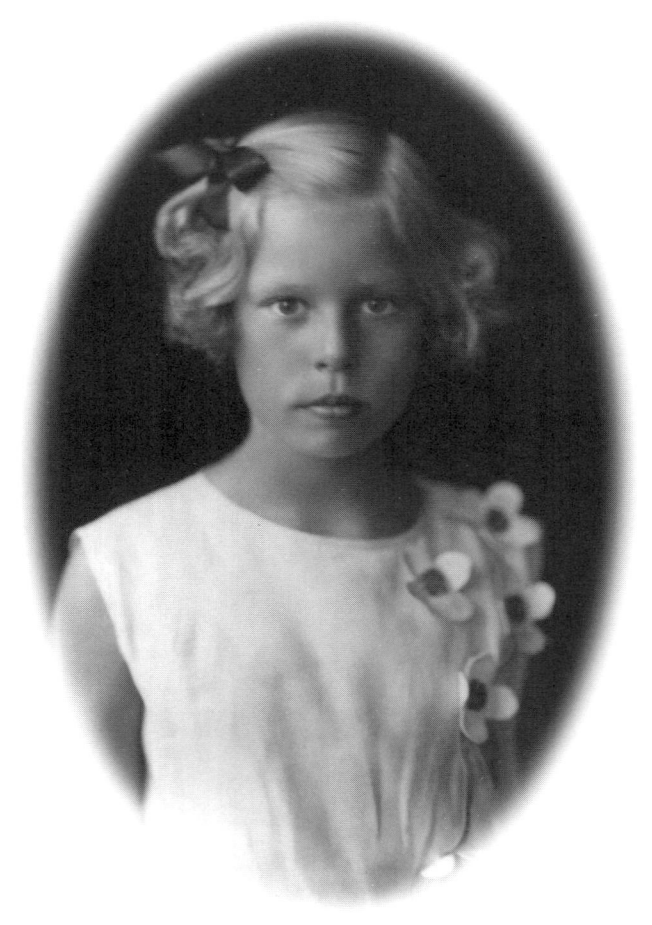

I AM A BROKEN RECORD

I'M NOT AFRAID;
JUST NOBODY WILL HIRE ME.
IT'S NOT MY FAULT.
IF MY PARENTS HAD GIVEN ME
THE TIME I NEEDED...
CAUGHT UP IN HAVING THINGS
WHEN THEY COULD OF HAD ME.

MY MOTHER SAYS SHE HATES ME.
I'M A BURDEN, A LEECH,
A BAD NIGHT OF SEX;
SHE NEVER MEANT TO COME.
NOTHING BUT MY FATHER'S FUCKING RAGE.
"LITTLE NO GOOD SHIT" SHE NAMED ME.
MY FATHER'S MOVED IN WITH ME;
NO ONE WILL HIRE HIM.
HE SAYS IT'S NOT HIS FAULT.
IF HIS FATHER HADN'T DONE HIM,
BURNED HIM, BROKE HIS NOSE...
HE'S DRUNK, UNSHAVED, IN LOVE WITH TV
EVEN WITHOUT CABLE.
"BOY, COME RUB MY FEET!"
SEEMINGLY HASN'T MOVED IN WEEKS.
 I WISH HE WAS DEAD.

TODAY I HEARD A WAIF OF A GIRL,
LOOKING LIKE SHE HADN'T A FRIEND
IN THIS WORLD,
SAY OVER AND OVER,
"I AM A BROKEN RECORD,
    I AM A BROKEN RECORD,
        I AM A BROKEN RECORD."
HER FACE IN THE CROWD DISAPPEARED.
I HEAR MYSELF, SOME SYMPATHY THERE.
"TOO FUCKING BAD, YOU LITTLE NO GOOD SHIT!"

The Fix

You leave nothing but yourself behind.
"Live your life as I intended."
Christ turns his head.

In a renegade church inhaling
Incense laden air,
Latin chants echo from icon-filled walls.
It was a mystery then, God's still a mystery now.
"Death is a terrible and frightful thing."
The voices of children, or is it angels, singing
"Teacher, teach us how to die."
The priest's eyes twinkle.
"Welcome to our little church. Hear for yourself the words
Once echoed within the walls of the catacombs themselves."
This requiem for a loved one.
Always searching, my prayers go out.

God, your voice resonates within me.
Lying here in this bed an addict in need,
Slowly injecting the faith into my veins,
Hoping the needle won't break.
The warm glow of the payoff, heaven surely brings.

BLACK HEART SHINING

Two pieces of walking toast
Stagger past;
Wiry frames moving towards some certain violent moment
Buttered by liquor or today's drug du jour.
Liquid eyes neither searching or focused on
The one-room sidewalk apartment. Crumpled before me
A sockless black foot,
The only human sign of its occupant,
Buried beneath a well-worn pile of clothing,
Fronted by a Schwinn Easy Rider bicycle
Like I had in my youth twenty-five years earlier.
Poor
As a point in time - a certain perspective.
The smell of crawfish etouffe and urban rhythms
Lure and linger.
Percolating topless women offer something from
Sun faded black and white stills. "Wash your favorite girl."
Dow Corning and rent payments flash through my head.
A child's small hand touching flesh,
The same flesh, suits and gin soaked louts
Leer at and covet. Putting bread on the table. Po-boys.
Amidst voodoo shops and fifteenth century furniture,
Louis Armstrong's head
Floats majestically, wailing on a silent trumpet.
I am mesmerized by all the things we are,
By all things human.
On Canal Street the final image,
Is Ernest Hemingway by Yousuf Karsh,
Not a picture but the actual photograph.
Eyes seeing a man who had really lived.

Oh, New Orleans- oh, mighty city by the Mississippi,
Hail to you and yours.

MY MOTHER'S LULLABY

The little toy dog is covered with dust,
But sturdy and staunch he stands.
The little tin soldier is covered with rust,
The musket molds in his hands.

Time was when little toy dog was new
And the soldier was standing fair,
And that was the time
When our little boy blue
Kissed them and put them there.

"Now don't you go till I come," he said,
"and don't you make any noise."
Then toddling off to his trundle bed
He dreamt of his sweet little toys.

And as he lay dreaming
An angel's song awakened our little boy blue.
Oh the years are many,
The years are long,
But his little toy friends are true.

Yes, the years are many,
The years are long,
But one thing will always hold true.
Know in your heart, when from this world I depart,
That I
Have always
Loved you.

Lullaby by Rita Rhein
Adapted from the original
Additional words by T. Rhein

DAY HEIGHTS, 1966

It was a day to be savored,
A memory that never fades.

Playing ball for my dad,
Learning I'd been traded.
"The other team has eight,"
He said, "It's you on their side or no game."
At first I cried, too sick to play.
You said, "Go on, take the field."
I could sense your pride.

Somehow I knew, Dad,
It was the last time
I'd look into your eyes
Full of anger and determination,
Flushed cheeks still not dry.
I swore I'd make you pay.
So I took the field to watch hit after hit.
It was only after five,
The ump called it quits.
Forty eight to six was that final score.
As I returned to the bench
You said, "It could have been more."
I wanted to punch you
But my arm was too sore, Dad.

It was the last time
I'd look into your eyes,
See them sparkle as you broke into that smile,
Telling me I tried,
That was all that really mattered.

Overcame my fears,
Took a big step up...
We walked out to the car,
Your hand on my shoulder.
We headed for the A&W Root Beer stand.
I felt like a star,
Perhaps a little older or maybe
Just more self assured.
I could see I could be more than
Just what I thought I could be.

Dad, it was the last time
I ever felt that close.
Thinking back now, the things I miss most
Are making you proud,
Showing you how I've grown,
The things I've gone on to achieve.
All because on that summer day
You gave up one of your own.

                        In memory of Jim Rhein Sr.

Photo by Kathleen Hume

HOMECOMING

Here from somewhere else
to see
a hometown measured by the years spent there.
I forget, myself, all the stories;
that sounded better coming from you anyway.
Somebody's on the porch.
I hear voices singing.
Smoke, beer, laughter, cards,
voices from the kitchen,
conversations about family
and those kids of ours.
Face to face to face...
Memories I've misplaced
or changed to fit the situation.
I'll tell you a story;
take it home with you.
I don't know the year,
it was the house on Melrose.
Grandpa Pete finds me sitting in a corner.
"Seems like you're always hiding or playing alone,
like you've got a secret."
I said, "I do."
He said, "Let me tell you something...
Everything's a dream when you're alone."
I said, "You're telling me to go play with the others."
He said, "Damn straight!" And he smiled at me.
I stand years later on the balcony
of that house
thinking about voices missing.
I miss Aunt Helen's talent show,
playing cards with Uncle Ed,
Grandma saying the rosary,
... and I really miss my dad.

Today, I tap into those roots,
draw on that fountain of truth
that keeps us all on the move.
Talk about old times,
and days yet to be...

I feel the joy and love of family.
I've come home.

THIS MOMENT

I sit.
thoughts struggle and turn,
small consolation,
life so vast.
Each day, each night, I yearn
for some understanding
of these things I've learned.
The morning sun rises.
A bird cries through the drifting fog.
I search in that call for the words.
In all the miles I have logged in this life
how seldom I have heard,
"I love you."
How often have I said it?
Is it too late?

Lying here now in this pain,
not knowing how many days remain.
Perhaps I can more clearly see
beyond my own personal tragedy.
Is it too late?

To take these children back in my arms,
to share my life's memories.
A special thought to keep them warm,
perchance to share their dreams.
To tell them what they've meant to me,
to tell them how much I believed in them.

To think of my wife,
sometimes the laughter and tears blur,
sometimes the years have not been kind;
but in all that silence
this love has survived.
And I do love you.

Tonight I just want to lie next to you;
please hold me in your arms.
I'm scared of letting go...
maybe you're scared too.

Try to look inside your heart to find
the boy you used to know,
the one who made sweet love to you
and swore he'd never let you go.
Think back to our wedding day,
when you glowed in God's own light,
a radiance that filled my heart
when you became my beautiful bride.
Store in your heart
a memory upon which to call.

I had fallen into a deep sleep,
God's angels were waiting at the gate.
"I don't want to depart this earth,
To leave her angry, sad, lonely.
What message can I send her?"
They drew close,
put their arms around me.
We began to walk
and I heard one tell me.

"Remember the secret of love,
we never lose someone we're a part of."

I go now where eagles soar,
knowing my life with you
was my beautiful reward.

BEAUTY AND SADNESS

Big, open grass field wavering with the wind.
An ocean of summer breezes.
His head rises, darting
as if he could catch it.
So free to play.
And I call his name,
Isaac!

He laughs.
There is a place in my heart
when it rains,
I can't explain it...
beauty and sadness.

The day begins with a lick on my palm.
A memory taste,
a place or time I see.
I tell these blues to go away;
they obey
the ritual of my feelings.

There's a place in my heart
when it rains,
I can't explain it...
The tears in my eyes,
yesterday's good-bye.
There's a beauty and sadness to this world.
His ghost remains.

Last night I dreamed
he was running through a lazy creek bed,
fur covered with dirt and muck;
I gave a whistle...

MY MISTAKE.
IN MOMENTS WE TWO WERE ONE,
HIS TONGUE WAGGING.
I WAS BATHED IN FUR, DIRT AND MUD
AND I SWEAR HE LOOKED ME IN THE EYE
AND WE LAUGHED.

I AWOKE TO FIND TEARS HAD LEFT A PATH.

THERE'S A PLACE IN MY HEART
WHERE HE WILL REMAIN,
OUR YEARS TOGETHER;
I LOVED HIM FROM THE START.
TIME TOOK HIM AWAY;
FROM THIS EARTH HE'S DEPARTED.
BUT SOMEDAY WE MAY MEET AGAIN AND
THAT OLD DOG AND I WILL PLAY.

WATCHING HIM CHASE THE WIND
AS HE DARTS THROUGH THAT OPEN FIELD,
IT IS WITH THIS WISH MY HEART IS HEALED;
AND I SAY HIS NAME,
ISAAC!

WHEN YOU GO

I see all your bags packed,
including all thirteen pairs of shoes.
This time must be for real
'cause even the toothpaste is wearing its cap.
I guess I find myself feeling blue.
When you go
can I come too?

You said you're sick and tired of
who I am.
Decent, hard working, and loving
is not your kind of man.
You said I always promised the gutter,
now we're living in Malibu
with two cars and a chihuahua.
Honey, I suppose that's all true.
But when you go
can I come too?

Love was so much easier
when we were too drunk to see it.
Passed out in each others' arms
in clothes made in Korea.
Viewing for dollars in sleaze bag bars
a table dance for two
who know who they are.

The engine is running.
I see your wig pinned to your head.
Chewing gum and smoking,
thinking about something witty I said.
You roll down the window,
flash me one of your smiles -
"See you in Hell, Lyle."
That's probably true.

Oh, baby, when you go
can I come too?
When you go
can I come too?

Replace Moments

There's a rose in the garden
eating up that rich loam.
There's a worm fixing up that dinner
and I'm sitting here alone.
Cross Chesapeake, Fourth and Main
there's a five and dime.
We used to sit there every day,
the corner seat by the coffee stain,
laughing, carrying on, having a good time.
We were the best when we were together,
so few friends like you and I.
There's a storm brewing over Selma;
the train whistle still carries your good-bye.

In 1942 it was the thing to do,
especially if you had no answers.
Young and loyal to the red, white, and blue
got you closer to the dancers.
I held you in my arms,
I knew only for this moment.
I still remember your touch.
We didn't know what the future held in store;
at the time it didn't seem to matter,
I was in love with your heart
that bullet shattered.

I hear the snipping shears,
that rose sits in a vase.
The mounted bass caught with that worm,
its look so cold and fierce.
This old dog sits curled at my feet.
The glitter in my eyes, liquid lost years.
It's 4 o'clock, the same every day,
always right on time,
the clicking and ringing of the crossing gate.
The whistle still carries your good-bye.

IL POSTINO

Sitting is silence
I watch as she looks.
The light like myself
attaches itself to her.
The woman is open,
still she sits thinking.
Magnet or passion, I am drawn towards her.
The scent of morning.
Sounds of life living
unconcerned with my thoughts or hers.
As I stand wishing
for just one moment
I could capture
the feel of her fingers
caressing her whispers.
The window is open
and I am still dreaming.

EARLENE

I never noticed
the soft light view.
Seventy seven smiles
and they were all from you.

I sense you most in springtime
with that wavering wind.
Just about closing time,
I begin again.

With these pictures of you
it's all we've ever been...
black and white nights,
colored days of unlived dreams.

Now I'm holding you so tight,
as if you'd slip away...
Another memory that might.
Unspoken words could only say
it was as it seems.

I still love you to this day.

When Gone is Forgotten

Missing the fingers on his right hand,
Self-consciously I notice.
I notice more than he does.
Who suffered the greater loss?

The angel Gabriel
Sporting dread locks, army fatigues
Sips from a bottle of Wild Irish Rose.

"Don't pity what you don't understand."

The intimacy of poverty.
Street level charity
Walks very quickly.
Money as some measure of caring,
Some duty performed.
Thinking,
Dust only exists to satisfy
Our compulsive need to remove it,
To feel better about ourselves.

I remember touching the hem of his garment.
He handed me back my change.
"You in far worse shape than me, buddy."

Photo by Chris Schurman

THE BARBERSHOP QUARTET

"What can I do for you?"
His hands begin to move over my head
snip, snip talking in code.
Storytellers with combs & scissors.
We the sheep, bleat our responses
"Yeah, uh-huh, is that so?"

OCTOBER'S STORY

"NOTHING ON YOUR BODY IS CENTERED.
  NOT YOUR EARS,
    OR YOUR EYES,
      OR A WOMAN'S BREAST,
        KNOW WHAT I MEAN?" HE CHUCKLES.
"THAT'S WHY YOUR SIDEBURNS
  ARE UNEVEN 'CAUSE
    YOUR EARS DON'T MATCH."
"EVER TRY TO MAKE ONE OF THEM BOWL CUTS
  MATCH UP - JESUS - AND THIS ONE GUY
HAS ME CUT ONE SIDEBURN COMPLETELY OFF
  LEAVING THE OTHER SIDE BELOW HIS EAR.
    HE INSISTS.
DRESSES REAL NICE, ONE OF THOSE HIGH IQ GUYS -
  NO, REALLY."
(I GUESS MY EYES BETRAYED SOME SIGN OF DOUBT
  THOUGH I DON'T REMEMBER EVEN MOVING.)
"SAYS IT'S TO PROTEST ALL THOSE LONG-HAIRED HIPPIE TYPES
  FROM THE SIXTIES; JEEZ, IT'S THE NINETIES -
THIRTY YEARS OF TWISTED LOGIC."
  (I HEAR A QUICK INHALE.)
"I THINK HE'S GOT IT BACKWARDS -
HE WAS PROBABLY ANTI-ESTABLISHMENT,
  ONE TOO MANY ACID TRIPS."
"FINISHED. WHAT DO YOU THINK?"

I THINK THERE IS NO CENTER
    TO MY LIFE-
NOTHING TO MAKE ME UNBALANCE MY SIDEBURNS
    TO MATCH MY POLITICS.

JANUARY'S STORY

"Where's Tom been?"
Tucks the apron round my collar.
"Tom's real sick,
  cancer, no insurance;
us barbers have to provide our own.
No Blue Cross-Blue Shield, no HMO."
"P & G, the regular, right?
  Off the ears - blocked cross the back?"
"Right."
  "Yeah, old Tom's real sick, not sure if
    he'll be back."
And I notice the new guy - I guess
  no time or reason
    for an empty chair.
Yet my sensibilities are offended,
  selfishly I guess.
See, of all the barbers
  only Tom had not cut my hair.
I feel cheated.
  Leaving the chair I put a twenty in the
  collection basket-
The sign said;
"Tom's only way to make a living."

MAY'S STORY

"You know, it's hard to know what to say sometimes."
Snip, snip.
"Like at funerals,
Or to someone who's been fired.
Or your best friends tell you they're getting divorced."
"Trim your eyebrows?"
"Just the wild ones."
"You know what I mean? Like this guy
sits here in the chair
and tells me his daughter,
who plays soccer with my girl Mindy,
has charged him with molesting her."
"I'm thinking, Jesus Christ, what do I say?"
(I say nothing.)
"He says, 'I feel sick - I love my daughter.
We've had our fights but I don't understand
why she'd want to do this.
My wife moved out.'"
"He says, 'Do you know how people react when they hear this?'"
(I'm thinking, yeah, Joel.. Just take a look in the mirror at me.)
"He said to me,
 'I feel dirty, like I have leprosy
  and all you have is your word,
   who you've been, who you are.
People won't look at you,
stop talking when you approach them.
Think they're talking 'bout you
 even when they're not.
Won't return your phone calls.'"
"I just let him talk, I didn't know what to say."
 (Me either.)
"Trim your sideburns?"
 "Sure, go ahead."
"You know, it's not often a barber's got nothing to say."

SEPTEMBER'S STORY

"Life demands to be lived."
He sprays the bottle, wets down my hair.
 Mirrors hanging in front and back of me,
Tom becomes moT.
I comment on them, the mirrors.
 "Let me tell you,
  there's this little guy, cute as a button—
blonde hair, cute as a button—
hates to have his hair cut.
He's crying, 'no mama, I don't want to
no-o-o!'
 She puts him in the chair.
Does that look, you know that look
 your mom gives you-
that, 'it's okay,' look - 'don't be afraid.'
He glances at me in the mirror.
 'Please Mr. Mot, don't change me too much.'
Of course I'd never thought of it that way.
People walk out of here with a whole different view of themselves,
 I make that happen." Tom smiles at me,
"Well, to get back to your original question,
 I just wasn't ready to go yet."

The Ones We Leave Behind

It's quiet here.
Time has no sound.
Beautiful beyond belief.

Faint smell of roses wafts by —
Great, I've already been signed on as God's gardener.
My hands feel touched.
My body floats on an ocean of light.
Is this the reward for having lived my life?
Is this what we search for?
The mystery unfolds.
No control of our beginnings,
No control of our end,
Just the time in between
Life and death.
Through the ones we leave behind
Our story gets told.

Do you remember the last thing I said?
Do you remember why we were friends?
Family?
Lovers?
The boom of my voice,
The shake of my hand,
The steeliness in my eyes when I was mad?
The tears I cried,
How I hated ties,
The word goodbye....

But Lord I loved to laugh.

I can't touch you now, the way I touched you then
So most of all I hope you'll remember when
I told you,
I love you.
I love you.

For Dan Grice. Peace to you brother.
4/8/97

THE BEST OF EVERYTHING

Poets, philosophers, those rooted in spirit
say life is a journey,
a quest, an adventure,
unpredictable as the weather.
That theory has merit
as much as any other,
and on my journey
so many people have stopped by to interact.
A stranger on the street
sees through the mask.
The stranger is the me;
I remember looking back.

To those who left their mark,
others so quickly forgotten.
Some of them I loved,
too many times those words left
unspoken.
Some who were mirrors -
our lives one long dance -
capturing me with their grace;
it's been an unending trance.
It's these folks I choose as
my roadmarkers in life,
to remember their style
when my legs are weary
and I don't want to carry on...

To keep reaching for dreams.
It's their voices in the night,
those angels singing.

"I wish you the best of everything."

I look down and notice my shoes
are still tied.

WHERE WILL I BE

On the day I was born
My father was practicing what he always preached,
"Never let life get in the way of business."
In the distance a barker called,
"Step right up to the biggest show in St. Paul."
My mother,
Worn out and tired, hummed along with the carousel.
A lullaby
That from the first day
Filled my ears with the rushing sounds of life.
Like a song
In my mind I'm stuck there,
Entranced by all the possibilities of happiness,
Of friendship
That ended every time the tent stakes got pulled up.
I cried,
Sometimes even now.

Looking back,
My upbringing was a tilt-a-whirl.
Daddy loved the whip,
That old trailer was the rock-o-plane,
Wires frying, sliding off track.
Sitting there with a fat lip, momma would always say,
"It's hard for your daddy to show his love."

But he sure loved the county fair,
The mix of humanity you could find there.
Those people would make him laugh.
I would see his eyes shine like he was really alive
Sometimes.
Mostly our spookhouse was haunted
By the ghost of Budweiser.
In the fun house mirror the old man's face
Showed a life stretched way too thin,
His clipped laugh masked a terror
I never could understand.

Have you ever seen the fears of a clown?
Is that my face now?

Like many carnival kids the road became
The only place that felt like home.
The comfort of a stranger's glance
Shatters the aching silence when
I feel alone.

My tires are balding,
So tired of running to stand still,
Yet I keep running
Always have, always will.

They say it's in the blood.
I see his face in the mirror
Same as it ever was,
Just now I have no excuse.

Tonight my head hit the pillow and I dreamed.
It wasn't a trailer, but a nice house
On Sycamore Street.

It had a real nice yard
Shaded by a big locust tree.
My daddy drove a Buick,
Worked the nine to five,
My momma's face was radiant, no black eye.
Jumping from his car, daddy
Lifted me into his arms.
"How's my little tiger?"

I awoke to the sounds of the big wheel turning.

      For John

About the Author

T. Rhein was born in Goshen, Ohio.
A graduate of Miami University with a degree
In education he has spent all of his adult life
Working in the Amusement Park business.
He considers himself a thoughtsmith more than a poet.
He currently lives in Cincinnati, Ohio.
All photos by T. Rhein except where noted.
Photographer unknown for pictures on pages 28 & 38.

T. RHEIN WOULD LIKE TO THANK THE FOLLOWING PEOPLE, WHO MADE THIS BOOK POSSIBLE.

MARGARET RHEIN, COVER ARTWORK "BLACK HEART SHINING" USED WITH HER PERMISSION. PHOTO CREDIT AS NOTED. ART DIRECTION.

KATHLEEN HUME, PHOTO DIRECTION. PHOTO CREDIT AS NOTED.

CHRIS SCHURMAN, PHOTO CREDIT AS NOTED. I HOPE THINGS ARE GOING WELL IN YOUR PART OF THE WORLD.

NORTON PHOTOGRAPHY STUDIOS

OTT COMMUNICATIONS, COVER DESIGN AND WORDS OF ENCOURAGEMENT.

TIM HOLT, FOR THE CALM DURING THE STORM.

STEVE CRAWFORD. SORRY ABOUT ALL THE CHANGES. THAT'S WHAT FRIENDS ARE FOR.

JOE TRAUTH, FOR THE EARS AND EYES.

CLIFF RADEL, FOR THE WORDS OF WISDOM.

MARY JO DILANARDO, FOR GETTING ME TO SHARE IN THE FIRST PLACE.

THE WALKERS, FOR THE OPPORTUNITY.

AND ESPECIALLY
JAN WELLER, A TRUE PARTNER IN CRIME.